I0136382

Frank Wallace Robinson

The Library of George W. Childs

Frank Wallace Robinson

The Library of George W. Childs

ISBN/EAN: 9783337816810

Printed in Europe, USA, Canada, Australia, Japan

Cover: Foto ©Thomas Meinert / pixelio.de

More available books at **www.hansebooks.com**

The Private Libraries of Philadelphia.

THE LIBRARY

OF

GEORGE W. CHILDS.

DESCRIBED BY

F. W. ROBINSON.

PHILADELPHIA:
COLLINS, PRINTER.
1882.

LIBRARY

OF

GEORGE W. CHILDS.

To Mr. CHILDS's life-long knowledge of books, and intimate personal acquaintance with celebrated authors at home and abroad, may be attributed the remarkable character of his collection. Its growth has been gradual, although the most curious portions have been obtained during the last fifteen years. The library contains about five thousand volumes. The room which is Mr. CHILDS's reading-room and study is upon the first floor, with direct entrance from the main hall of his mansion, and the woodwork is finished in the Italian style, carved ebony with gold. The book-shelves are on the four sides, and are six feet in height. The walls above are beautifully finished to the ceiling, which is built in heavy sunken panels, blue and gold. In the centre of the room stands the large

library table, literally piled with attractive
volumes. This table is in itself a treasure,
the ebony of which it is made having been
brought from Africa by M. Paul du Chaillu
for Mr. CHILDS. The furniture is of ebony,
and the library chair, also of ebony, is a fac-
simile of William Beckford's chair at Font-
hill. The carpet, of a unique design by
Owen Jones, corresponds with every part of
the room. The remainder of the books are
in an elegant apartment upon the third floor,
chiefly devoted to the standard works. These
include the finest editions of all the best
English and American authors, with many
specialties in various branches of literature.
To us, however, the greatest treasures are
those in the library-room first named. In
a beautiful cabinet between the windows
we find a little 18mo. of 8 pages, bearing the
date May 17, 1703, written in a small but
very clear hand, the lines close together, but
with wide margins for references. This is
an original sermon of the Rev. Cotton Mather,
endorsed as genuine by Rev. Wm. B. Sprague,
Albany.

We next come to a copy of the Poetical
Works of Leigh Hunt, also a little 18mo.
This is doubly precious from the associations
that cluster around it, the autograph inscrip-

tion being, "Charles Dickens, from his Constant Admirer and obliged friend, Leigh Hunt." It is the Moxon edition of 1844, is bound in half morocco, and came to Mr. CHILDS direct from Dickens's library. Accompanying this, and from the same library, is a copy of Hood's "Comic Annual" for 1842. Mr. Welford secured the work with considerable difficulty, as thirty-two applications were made for it by English collectors. The inscription, in Hood's handwriting, has never been published, but it is too good not to see the light. It is as follows:—

> Pshaw! away with leaf and berry,
>   And the sober-sided cup!
> Bring a goblet, and bright sherry!
>   And a bumper fill me up.
> Tho' I had a pledge to shiver,
>   And the longest ever was—
> Ere his vessel leaves our river,
>   I will drink a health to Boz!
>
> Here's success to all his antics,
>   Since it pleases him to roam,
> And to paddle o'er Atlantics,
>   After such a *sale* at home!—
> May he shun all rocks whatever,
>   And the shallow sand that lurks—
> And his passage be as clever
>   As the best among his works!
>   THOS. HOOD.

Here, also, is a beautiful octavo edition, full morocco, with a wonderfully delicate gold finish, of "Alnwick Castle and Other Poems," with the inscription in the poet's own hand—

Charles Dickens, Esquire,
from his friend and admirer,
FITZ GREENE HALLECK.
New York, North America,
6th June, 1842.

Another work attracts our attention, which proves to be the original manuscript of Nathaniel Hawthorne's Consular Experiences. It contains thirty-seven large quarto pages, is in the author's hand throughout, and has his signature at the end. It is remarkable for the beauty of its pages, its clean sheets, and its freedom from alterations and erasures. With it is a copy of the first edition of the "Scarlet Letter," published by Ticknor, Reed & Fields in 1851, containing an autograph letter to Mr. CHILDS, dated Lenox, September 16, 1851. We give it in full :—

MY DEAR SIR :—

Perhaps it may interest you to know that " The Scarlet Letter" (your favorable opinion of which gratifies me much) is thus far founded on fact, that such a symbol was actually worn by at least one woman, in the early times of New England. Whether this personage resembled Hester Prynne in any other circumstances of her character, I cannot say ; nor whether this mode of ignominious punishment was brought from beyond the Atlantic, or originated with the New England Puritans. At any rate, the idea was so worthy of them that I am piously inclined to allow them all the credit of it.

Respectfully,

NATHL. HAWTHORNE.

GEORGE W. CHILDS, Esq.

In connection with the above we read the sad letter written by Ex-President Pierce to James T. Fields, giving an account of the death of Mr. Hawthorne. It is in the book of the Presidents of the United States, to which we shall call attention later. It is written on a broad, square, black-edged sheet, and is as follows :—

PEMIGEWASSET HOUSE,
Thursday Morning, 5 o'clock.

MY DEAR SIR :—

The telegraph has communicated to you the fact of our dear friend Hawthorne's death. My friend, Col. Hibbard, who bears this note, was a friend of Hawthorne, and will tell you more than I am able to write. I enclose herewith a note which I commenced last evening to dear Mrs. Hawthorne. Oh, how will she bear this shock ! Dear mother—dear children. When I met Hawthorne at Boston, a week ago, it was apparent that he was much more feeble, and more seriously diseased, than I had supposed him to be. We came from Senter Harbor yesterday afternoon, and I thought he was on the whole brighter than he was the day before. Through the week he has been inclined to somnolency during the day, but restless at night. He retired last night soon after nine o'clock, and soon fell into a quiet slumber. In less than half an hour changed his position, but continued to sleep. I left the door open between his bed and mine, our beds being opposite to each other, and was asleep myself before 11 o'clock. The light continued to burn in my room. At 2 o'clock I went to H.'s bedside ; he was apparently in a sound sleep, and I did not place my hand upon him. At 4 o'clock I went into his room again, and, as his position was unchanged, I placed my hand upon him and found that life was extinct. I sent, however, immediately for a physician, and called Judge Bell and Col. Hibbard, who occupied rooms upon the same floor and near me. He lies upon his side—his position so perfectly natural and easy—his eyes closed—that it is difficult to realize while looking upon his noble face that this is death. He must have passed from natural slumber to that from which there is no waking within the slightest moment.

I cannot write to dear Mrs. Hawthorne, and you must exercise your judgment with regard to sending this and the unfinished note enclosed to her.

Yr. Friend
FRANKLIN PIERCE.

The manuscript of another author who is dear to the American reader, and who has but lately passed away, is William Cullen Bryant's It is in quarto form, and contains the First Book of the Iliad. There are sixteen pages, and a vignette portrait on steel, one of the best we have ever seen of the poet. Accompanying it is an autograph letter to Mr. Fields :—

My DEAR Mr. FIELDS :—

I send you the first half of the First Book of the Iliad translated by me, relating the contention between Achilles and Agamemnon. If it be desirable that I should see the proof, it should be sent to me immediately, as I may possibly not be in these parts in about ten days from this time.

I am, Dear Sir,
Very Sincerely Yours,
W. C. BRYANT.

Roslyn, Nov. 6, 1866.

A nine-page folio, in manuscript, is James Russell Lowell's June Idyll, "Under the

Willows," signed "J. R. L." upon the title-page, and at the end with the full name of the poet. This poem was begun in 1850, and completed in 1868, but, despite the length of this period, the work exhibits few emendations.

A manuscript of interest is the original of James Fenimore Cooper's "Life of Captain Richard Somers," twenty-one pages folio, bound with the text as published in *Graham's Magazine*, October, 1847. This is bound in half morocco, and it was presented to Mr. Balmanno by Rufus W. Griswold, with his autograph attestation. In addition to the above, the volume contains ten autograph letters, signed, to J. D. P. Ogden, Esq., his lawyer, concerning his lawsuit against J. Watson Webb and others for libel, 1839–1840; also, an unsigned letter to the editor of the *Commercial Advertiser*, with notes and newspaper cuttings inserted by Mr. Balmanno.

A singular history is attached to a remarkable manuscript to be found here, that of "The Murders in the Rue Morgue," by Edgar A. Poe. The story is complete on seventeen pages of large folio paper, the handwriting being small and close. There are very few alterations, and the letters are clean and clear. The story of the manuscript can be best understood by the following, which accompanied it when it came into Mr. CHILDS's possession :—

The foregoing original manuscript of Edgar A. Poe's story, "The Murders in the Rue Morgue," has a history which may be of interest to admirers of the distinguished author. I have no data whereby I can fix the exact date at which the manuscript came into my possession, but it was *about* forty years ago, probably in the spring of 1841, at which time I was an apprentice in the office of Barrett & Thrasher, Printers, No. 33 Carter's Alley, Philadelphia. If my memory is not at fault, *Graham's Magazine*, in whose pages the story first appeared, was printed in the aforesaid office, and the revised proof read in the *Saturday Evening Post* office, Chestnut Street above Third, within a door or two of the old *Public Ledger* building.

After the story had been put in type and the proof read, the manuscript found its way into the waste-basket. I picked it from the basket, asked and obtained leave to keep it, and took it to the residence of my father, with whom I then boarded. Here it was put away so carefully that I have no recollection of seeing it for years.

In 1846, my father, leaving me in Philadelphia, removed to Fawn Township, York County, and thence, a few years later, to Manchester, Md., and Darksville, Va. In these several pilgrimages he had, unknown to himself, carried the Poe manuscript along with him, folded up in one of the books of his library. Determining to return to Pennsylvania, he made sale of his personal effects, and among a lot of old books offered was found the Poe MS. It was at once recognized, rescued from the rubbish among which it had so nearly been lost, and forwarded to me—I having in the mean time, 1847, removed to Lancaster, Pa., and commenced business as a daguerreotypist. Twice my daguerrean rooms took fire, and once (March 8, 1850) almost all my books, papers, pictures, and apparatus were consumed; but the Poe manuscript, folded within the leaves of an old music book, escaped the wreck.

About the year 1857 (I think it was), a grocery store, occupying the first floor of the building in which were my rooms, took fire and burned furiously. The flames did not reach my rooms, but the smoke did, and the firemen drenched them with water, destroying books, papers, and other property, but, by rare good fortune, the Poe manuscript again escaped all injury, except a slight discoloration.

From 1861 to 1864 I was in the army, but, on my return therefrom, I found the Poe manuscript in the old music book where I had left it on leaving home.

In the spring of 1865 I took charge of the Swan Hotel, Lancaster. Removing therefrom in 1869, a great deal of rubbish was consigned to the ash-pile, the old music book sharing the fate of other worthless articles. My next-door neighbor, thinking it had been inadvertently thrown away, picked it from the ash-pile and handed it to me. On opening the book, I again beheld the much-neglected and long-mislaid manuscript ! Resolved that it should not again be subjected to so many unnecessary risks, I at once had it bound in its present form.

J. W. JOHNSTON.

Lancaster, Pa., July 26, 1881.

Another interesting memento in connection with the history both of this manuscript and its unfortunate author is given below :

MESSRS. LEA & BLANCHARD,—

PHILADELPHIA.

Gentlemen : I wish to publish a new collection of my prose Tales with some such title as this :—

   ‘ *The Prose Tales of Edgar A. Poe, including*
    “ *The Murders in the Rue Morgue,*” *the*
    “ *Descent into The Maelström,*” *and all*
    his later pieces, with a second edition of the
    “ *Tales of the Grotesque and Arabesque.*” ’

The later pieces will be eight in number, making the entire collection thirty-three, which would occupy two *thick* novel volumes.

I am anxious that your firm should continue to be my publishers, and, if you would be willing to bring out the book, I should be glad to accept the terms which you allowed me before, that is, you receive all profits, and allow me twenty copies for distribution to friends.

Will you be kind enough to give me an early reply to this letter, and believe me

Yours, very respectfully,

EDGAR A. POE.

Philadelphia,
Office Graham's Magazine, August 13, '41.

From this it would appear that Mr. Poe was at least modest in his demands upon his publishers.

It was principally through Mr. CHILDS's instrumentality that the monument to Poe was erected in Baltimore, as he volunteered to pay all the expenses attending it, and did furnish the greater part of the money.

Of great historical value is the original manuscript draft of General U. S. Grant's Address at the opening of the Centennial Exhibition, May 10, 1876. It is in full, and signed by him. Mr. CHILDS has had it elegantly bound in full morocco folio, with blue satin lining.

Probably the unique work in Mr. CHILDS's whole collection is the original manuscript of "Our Mutual Friend," which he has had bound in two large quarto volumes, fine brown morocco. It is the only complete manuscript of any of Charles Dickens's novels outside the South Kensington Museum. It is said, however, that one or two of his short Christmas stories are to be found in this country and in England.

The manuscript is dated "Thursday, Fourth January, 1866," and is signed, at the head of the sheet, "Charles Dickens." Then comes the skeleton of the story. The method Mr. Dickens pursued in the construction of his novels may not be known; and a brief description of it will to some extent explain the skeleton from which we shall give a few extracts. In the first place the author conceived a plan of his story, then thought it out carefully, and fixed the plot firmly in his mind, together with the salient traits of each character. This completed, he made his skeleton, from which to work in the details; and then came the detailed work of the book. We copy from the first part of Volume I.

OUR MUTUAL FRIEND, NO. 1.

CHAPTER I.

ON THE LOOKOUT.

The Man, in his boat, watching the tides.
The Gaffer,—Gaffer—Gaffer Hexam—
　　Hexam. .
His daughter rowing.　Jen, or Lizzie.
Taking the body in tow.
His dissipated partner,　　　　　　　who
　　has "Robbed a live man!"
Riderhood—this fellow's name.

CHAPTER II.

THE MAN FROM SOMEWHERE.

The entirely new people.
Everything new—Grandfather　new—if they
　　had one.
Dinner Party—Twemlow, Podsnap, Lady Tip-
　　pins, Alfred Lighthouse, also Eugene—Mor-
　　timer, languid and tells of Harmon the Dust
　　Contractor.

Then come sentences like this: "Work
in the girl who was to have been married
and made rich," etc.　These are written in
diagonally, vertically, or horizontally, as the
case may be.　There is also an outline head-
ing, as follows:—

FOUR BOOKS.

I. The Cup and the Lip.
II. Birds of a Feather.
III. A Long Lane.
IV. A Turning.

The skeleton, of which we have given a slight idea, covers nearly sixteen quarto pages. Following this is the text of the work itself.

The paper used is light blue and heavy; and the ink is dark blue. Mr. Dickens wrote a peculiar hand, the lines very close together, the letters very small; and the frequent marks of erasure and change betray the utmost care in the preparation of his work. At times a whole line has been scored out, to be replaced by another choice of words or a different mode of expression, or to be dropped altogether. Occasionally evidences of the author's entire absorption in his work may be seen in the departure of the lines from exactness, and their tendency towards the corners of the sheet. It is not difficult to form a mental picture of the self-forgetfulness of the great writer, and of his utter abandonment to his work, as he sits at his library table at Gads Hill hour after hour, weaving the threads of his wonderful stories.

*

In the second volume the same method is observed, the skeleton occupying eighteen similar pages, in which there is an extra note to suggest something regarding Mr. Boffin.

The story is marked as completed September 2, 1865, and has a postscript in lieu of a preface, occupying about one and one-third page, under which is given this date. The manuscript is just as it came finally from Mr. Dickens's hands, even the names of the compositors in the printing-office remaining at the head of each "take."

In the first volume is inserted a letter from Mr. Dickens to Mr. CHILDS.

GADS HILL PLACE,
Higham by Rochester, Kent.
Wednesday, Fourth November, 1868.

MY DEAR MR. CHILDS :

Welcome to England ! Dolby will have told you that I am reading again—on a very fatiguing scale—but that after the end of next week, I shall be free for a fortnight as to country readings. On Monday next I shall be in town, and shall come straight to pay my respects to Mrs. Childs and you. In the mean time will you, if you can, so arrange your engagements as to give me a day or two here in the latter half of this month ? My housekeeper-daughter is away hunting in Hampshire, but my sister-in-law is always in charge.

and my married daughter would be charmed to come from London to receive Mrs. Childs. You cannot be quieter anywhere than here, and you certainly cannot have from any one a heartier welcome than from me.

With kind regards to Mrs. Childs,

Believe me,

Faithfully Yours Always,

CHARLES DICKENS.

GEORGE W. CHILDS, Esquire.

The envelope containing the above is a memento that would be a treasure to many, the great novelist's autograph appearing upon it as follows.—

GEORGE W. CHILDS, ESQUIRE,

Langham Hotel,

Regent Street,

London, West.

CHARLES DICKENS.

The same volume also contains a letter from Miss Mamie Dickens, of seven pages, dated February 6th, 1874, giving an account of the family and their movements.

Another curiosity is the fine Osgood edition of Dickens's works, in fifty-six volumes, bound in light half calf, very handsome, in each volume of which is inserted an autograph letter from **Mr.** Dickens to **Mr.** Childs, the first dated 1855.

Lord Byron's works are represented by Murray's fine six-volume edition, superbly bound, dated 1855, in which is to be found this inscription written by Mr. Murray :—

To George W. Childs, of Philadelphia,
In testimony of kind remembrance,
from
John Murray,
Albemarle Street, London.

The first volume contains portions of the manuscript of the "Bride of Abydos," and is signed by Lord Byron. An additional signature of note is that of "John Murray III., April, 1873." Byron's dislike of Wordsworth is well known, and when "Peter Bell" appeared, he cut it out, placed it in the beginning of a copy of his own works, and wrote a parody upon it, the manuscript verses occupying the margins of the page. This is also inserted in the first volume. Wordsworth's poem begins as follows :—

PROLOGUE.

There's something in a flying horse,
  And something in a huge balloon ;
But through the clouds I'll never float
Until I have a little Boat
  Whose shape is like the crescent-moon.

And now I *have* a little Boat,
In shape a very crescent-moon :—etc.

Byron expresses his extreme disgust in
these lines :—

Ravenna, March 22, 1820.
BYRON.

EPILOGUE.

There's something in a stupid ass,
  And something in a heavy dunce ;
But never since I went to school
I heard or saw so damned a fool
  As William Wordsworth is for once.

And now I've seen so great a fool
  As William Wordsworth is for once ;
I really wish that Peter Bell,
And he who wrote it, were in hell,
  For writing nonsense for the nonce.

I saw the " light in ninety-eight,"
  Sweet Babe of one-and-twenty years !
And then he gives it to the nation,
  And deems himself of Shakspeare's peers.

He gives the perfect work to light !
Will Wordsworth—if I might advise,
  Content you with the praise you get
  From Sir George Beaumont, Baronet,
And with your place in the Excise.

The fifth volume of this edition is accompanied by a fine line engraving from the finest portrait of Byron known, the original of which hangs in Mr. Murray's house, and to which is affixed an autograph of Lord Byron.

Mr. Cꜱ ʟᴅꜱ has also in his possession Lord Byron's writing-desk, on which he wrote Don Juan and other of his Poems. It has his autograph and notes in several places, as well as his crest and monogram.

A very handsome manuscript by William Godwin next attracts attention. It is the original of " Cloudesley : a Novel." Throughout it is the author's work, written on old parchment paper, upon both sides of the sheet. The chirography is particularly clear and smooth, and the large margin left for notes gives each page a tasteful appearance. The manuscript is bound in half calf, and each leaf is mounted on a strong guard.

A curiosity, indeed, is the book which has the following title-page :—

LA
DIVINA COMMEDIA
DI
DANTE
EDIZIONE ILLUSTRATA
da 30 Fotografie tolte da disegni
di
SCARAMUZZA

—

MILANO
ULRICO HOEPLI
1879

It is the smallest book ever printed, and is what the printer would denominate a "128mo." It contains the whole of Dante's Comedy, and the illustrations are clear and excellent. Mr. Hoepli, whose autograph appears on the dedicatory page, printed only a few copies for the Paris exhibition of 1878, and the types were destroyed after having been used on this occasion. The little volume measures, bound in full Turkey gilt, less than two and a quarter inches in length by one and a half inch in width, and yet it contains over five hundred pages of type that can be read with comparative ease by the naked eye.

Unequalled in its present shape is the manuscript of "The Cow Chace," which in any case would be of interest. It will be remembered that this satirical poem, written by Major André, was founded upon an unsuccessful attempt of a party under General Anthony Wayne to capture a block-house upon the Hudson, in New Jersey, and but a short distance from New York City, on the 21st of July, 1780. It is said to have been the last literary effort of the ill-fated young Englishman, and, singular enough, the last canto was published in New York, in Rivington's *Royal Gazette*, on the same day upon which he was arrested. The Poem was afterwards printed, with full notes, for private circulation, and this with the manuscript was the property of the Rev. Wm B. Sprague, of Albany, N. Y., an extensive collector of autographs, who prized it as probably the most valuable article in his collection. The manuscript has been wonderfully well illustrated by Mr. Ferdinand J. Dreer, of Philadelphia, who has inserted an illustration for every point in the text that would admit of it. These include portraits of the Generals of the Revolution, both Continental and English, well known and historic landscapes, characters, and buildings. The closing strain of André's epic, which is complete in three cantos, is:—

And now I've closed my epic strain,
. And tremble as I show it,
Lest this same warrior-drover, Wayne,
Should ever catch the poet.

Sure enough, just afterward the poet was caught, and some unkind hand continues the movement :—

And when the epic strain was sung,
The poet by the neck was hung—
And to his cost he finds too late
The "dung-born tribe" decides his fate.

A book that has no duplicate—in fact, a duplicate to-day would be impossible to make—is what has become known as

A COLLECTION OF AUTOGRAPHS
MADE BY
A SCRIVENER.

Mr. W. G. Latham, a lawyer of New Orleans, was the compiler, and of him the friend to whom the book was dedicated writes :—

He is, by profession, a Notary Public; and, in this capacity, has had access to many original documents whence he commenced making copies of signatures : and he thus employed the leisure hours of five and twenty years; and probably made at least one journey to Europe.

The accuracy of the imitations has in many instances been proved by comparison with the identical originals—that method, alone, being the true method of comparison : for no one writes uniformly through a series of years.

No duplicates of these copies have been preserved : and if this collection should be lost or destroyed, no power could now reproduce it.

Every autograph in the volume, it must be borne in mind, was copied by Mr. Latham. None are the originals, and none are lithographs or engraved *fac-similes.* There are about four thousand names in the book, and they embrace distinguished Americans of all professions from the beginning ; British authors from before Shakspeare until within a few years ; men of renown in authorship, in medicine, theology, natural history, botany, music, the drama, and the fine arts ; a complete list of the Signers of the Declaration of Independence ; Washington and his Generals ; Napoleon and leading men of his time and nation ; and, finally, royalty, the nobility, and military and naval celebrities of Europe for the past three centuries. Appended to almost every signature is a brief biographical sketch, which greatly enhances the value of the work. A much thinner volume, but bound to match exactly,

and corresponding in size of page, is the
Index. In the first part of this is the "Index to the Index," which guides to the subject classification; then under each subject
is an alphabetical arrangement of the names.
It is so complete that in a moment one may
turn to any desired name or epoch.

Among the most recent additions to Mr.
CHILDS's library is what is known as "The
Hall Collection." This aggregation of valuable material embraces letters, manuscripts,
and sketches from the most celebrated people
of the last fifty years, which were received
by Anna Maria Hall and her husband, Mr.
S. C. Hall, chiefly during their connection
with the *London Art Journal*.

Possessing, perhaps, the greatest general
interest in the Hall Collection, however, is
the album formerly belonging to Mrs. Hall,
now the property of Mr. CHILDS. Not only
do we find in it, almost without number,
names which everybody knows in English literature, many accompanying original
verses or bright sayings, but here and there
are sketches by well-known hands, sometimes in water-colors, sometimes in sepia,
sometimes in ink. There are letters from
Charles Lamb, Nathaniel Hawthorne, Mary
Somerville, Miss Mitford, Harriet Martineau,

Martin Farquhar Tupper, Robert Chambers,
S. T. Coleridge, Frederika Bremer, Samuel
Lover. Wilkie Collins, William Wordsworth,
Daniel O'Connell, Amelia Opie, Robert
Southey, L. H. Sigourney, Edward Lytton
Bulwer, E. B. Browning, from Rome, G.
P. R. James, Robert Burns, Grace Aquilar,
and many others. Will. Kennedy has a
Moorish Melody; T. Crofton Croker has a
sketch in sepia; Tom Moore has lines of
remembrance, and a sketch of Sloperton Cottage; there is also a page of manuscript
from one of his stories, written by Charles
Dickens, and signed with that never-to-be-forgotten signature. Under this he has written, "Countersigned, Boz." An interesting
sepia sketch of Maria Edgeworth's library
appears; and following it is "The Cross," a
poem by Jane Porter. Thomas Hood has
written a verse of his "Song of the Shirt,"
and Thomas Hood, the younger, presents
the lines beginning "Work, work, work."
There is "A Prayer" by Hannah More;
and Barry Cornwall comes soon after with
"A Conceit." Leigh Hunt writes nearly a
page of Abou Ben Adhem, and Caroline
Norton has "A Blind Man's Bride." Two
neat charades must not be overlooked, under

which is to be seen the signature of Theodore
Hook.

From Mrs. Hall, though perhaps not
strictly to be included in the Hall Collection, is "The Tom Moore Bible." The following, which is from Mrs. Hall, and which
accompanies the book, will, no doubt, serve
as the best description of its value.

AVENUE VILLA.
50 Holland Street,
Kensington, W. London.

This Bible, in which Thomas Moore had en-
tered the names, and birth dates, and death
dates of his children, was left by his widow,
"Bessy" Moore, to her nephew, Charles Murray. By him it was left to his widow, who presented it to Mrs. S. C. Hall as a very precious
relic.

By Mrs. S. C. Hall it is presented—on the 13th
day of October, 1879—to GEORGE W. CHILDS, of
Philadelphia, an honored and much loved citi-
zen of the United States of America, as the best
and most valuable offering she could make to
him, as a grateful tribute of respect, regard, and
esteem.

Curious, as well as rare, is the "Black
Book of Taymouth," a square quarto, very
handsome even as to its external appearance,
the binding being a rich black calf with all

the tooling in clear gold. This volume was presented to Mr. CHILDS by the Duke of Buckingham, the last of the Plantagenets, and contains his letter asking its acceptance. The book was printed for private circulation by the Marquis of Breadalbane, who was a relative of the Duke of Buckingham. It contains the "Black Book of Taymouth," which is superbly illustrated in the olden style, with brilliant coloring and much gold, and the text of which is in old English. It also contains a fine engraving of Taymouth Castle and a number of papers from the Breadalbane Charter-Room, and is replete with interesting material connected with this genealogical history. A superbly bound folio volume of photographs of Stowe, also sent to Mr. CHILDS by the Duke of Buckingham, serves as an interesting memorial of pleasant days spent with the Duke and his family in that famous lordly palace.

The "Memento of Dean Stanley," whose recent visit to this country and as the guest of Mr. CHILDS will be so well remembered, will be a lasting memorial of that great and good man. It contains two portraits of the Dean, one a full length study, and several letters from him to Mr. CHILDS. A fine reproduction, colored, of "The Herbert-Cowper Memorial Window," presented by Mr. CHILDS to Westminster Abbey also has a place, and all the letters and articles relating to the proposed monument to the Dean are to be found in the volume.

A valuable reminiscence is "The Need of Two Loves," the original manuscript of N. P. Willis. It occupies comparatively few pages; but the student of character-penmanship would find it, in its changes of form, an interesting bit of study.

Mr. CHILDS is the fortunate possessor of the original copy of Milton's "Paradise Lost," in Armenian, which was exhibited at the World's Fair in London. It was translated by the Rev. Dr. Pakradouny, and is a superb specimen of letterpress. It contains several original illustrations, including a fine portrait of Queen Victoria, to whom the work is dedicated.

Another work is the manuscript of "Hertha," by Frederika Bremer, translated by Mary Howitt. It bears date 1856, Stockholm, and the work is written by the author upon both sides of the sheet. The writing is smooth and flowing, and quite distinct. The MS. is in fine condition, and has been bound in a style worthy of its talented author.

By its side is the manuscript copy of Harriet

Martineau's "Retrospect of Western Travel," in four quarto volumes, with portraits taken in 1833 and 1850. The sheets are in excellent condition, and it is fascinating to read in her own hand the expression of her thoughts.

A unique book is a copy of Gray's Works, in two volumes, quarto, bound in tree calf. Originally it had but four illustrations, but it is enriched by the addition of one hundred and fourteen engravings and two drawings, and by autograph letters of Dr. Beattie, Sir Egerton Brydges, and others. It has an extra title-page marked as sold by the *author*, giving place and street. It is 18mo. in size, and was printed in London in 1797. Bound up in the work is the "Habitations of our Kings," an original manuscript of the poet Gray, covering four closely written quarto pages, and embracing the time from William the Conqueror to the Georges. It gives accounts of the Tower, the castles, and other old landmarks, so many of which are now destroyed or changed.

In presentation copies Mr. CHILDS's library is particularly rich, there being works from many of the leading authors of England and America during the last twenty-five years, each containing the autograph of the author.

Among these is a copy of the "Autocrat of the Breakfast-Table," from Dr. Holmes, which contains an interesting letter giving the author's reasons for beginning the papers in the *Atlantic Monthly*. A complete set of Longfellow's works is enriched with autograph letter in each volume.

The book which to most Americans would be fraught with the greatest interest, however, is a large folio containing the portrait of every President of the United States, from George Washington to General Chester A. Arthur. Upon the leaf following each portrait is an autograph letter from the President represented. The letters begin with the last letter General Washington ever wrote, which is dated "Mount Vernon, 8th December, 1799," six days before his death. A curious fact comes to light, resulting from the collection of these documents. It is that of the entire list the most difficult letter to be procured was that of President Andrew Johnson. Johnson's letters written by an amanuensis and *signed* by himself are easy to obtain; but so rare is a letter written *throughout* by him that as high as fifty dollars have been offered for one. The letter in this book covers eight pages, and is written in Mr. Johnson's incisive style. President Lincoln's letter is the celebrated one of instructions to General McClellan, which occupies four large quarto pages, and in which he says forcibly, "But you must *act!*" Franklin Pierce's letter has already been referred to in connection with the death of Hawthorne. Opposite General Grant's portrait is the noted letter from London, which was published throughout the world, giving his opinion of his hearty and enthusiastic reception in England. Six of these letters are personal ones from the Presidents to Mr. CHILDS. We have not space to refer in detail to all the letters, but from those we have mentioned the character of the whole can be readily judged.

Of especial importance to Shakspearian scholars is Mr. CHILDS's copy of Mrs. Mary Cowden Clarke's "Complete Concordance to Shakspeare." This interesting volume contains a selection of upwards of fifty closely written pages of the original manuscript, together with a long and exceedingly interesting autograph letter signed (10 pp.). It gives a minute and detailed account of the progress of the work from its inception, through the twelve years occupied in its compilation, and four more of press corrections, to its final publication. Also, copies of a congratulatory letter from Douglas Jerrold; the author's application for the privilege of dedicating the work to the Queen ; and the Queen's reply ; besides several portraits, and a large number of newspaper cuttings, etc., all neatly mounted. The author gives the following account of the origin of a Shakspearian Concordance :—

One fine morning, the 15th of July, 1829, at the table of some friends in Somersetshire, the subject of Cruden's Concordance to the Bible was started, its vast utility discussed, and a regret expressed that no work existed for the quoters of Shakspeare. The hope of facilitating the use of his universal axioms, of helping to spread still further the knowledge of his wondrous wisdom and truth, fired my ambition ; the desire to be myself the means of supplying a concordance to the Bible of the Intellectual World, seized upon my imagination. That very day I began my glorious task ; with a pencil and the *Tempest* in my hand, I accompanied my friends in their morning walk, thus offering the first lines of my work in honor of Nature's poet on Nature's own shrine—in the face of Nature herself—in the open air.

This is followed by a letter to Mr. CHILDS, which we present below :—

VILLA NOVELLO, GENOA,
8th Feb. 1879.

DEAR SIR :—

The more than kind reception you gave my letter of 2d November last (acknowledging your packet and sending you a copy of my memoir of my dear and honored father) in the shape of that truly cordial notice of our books in your Public Ledger Supplement for 23d November, 1878, induces me to believe that you will feel some interest in looking through the enclosed Prospectus of the last Shakspearian work my beloved Husband and I wrote together.

The notice in your paper was read through tears of proud emotion at the way in which your reviewer recognized the admirable characters of my Parents: It was enjoyed in concert by our family party, then assembled around our breakfast-table here; which included my brother Alfred, my sister Sabilla, and our two charming Italian nieces, Portia and Valeria Gigliucci—to whom I read aloud, as well as my streaming eyes would allow me, this American warmth of tribute to Vincent and Mary Novello's moral and intellectual excellence.

With heartfelt thanks, I am, my dear sir,
Yours, faithfully and gratefully obliged,
MARY COWDEN CLARKE.

GEORGE W. CHILDS; Esq.

The manuscript pages in the Concordance are in Mrs. Clarke's handwriting, and show in detail the method of work in the preparation of the volume.

A book to interest every one is Mrs. CHILDS's own album. In appearance it is very unpretentious, though handsome, but its covers contain what it would be impossible to duplicate—the names of the guests who have accepted the hospitality of Mr. and Mrs. CHILDS at their homes in Philadelphia, Long Branch, and Wootton. The first name to be seen is that of U. S. Grant, and this is followed by the names of the other members of the general's family. The signatures embrace those of the ablest men in every profession. Among literary men represented are Longfellow, Holmes, W. W. Story, Wilkie Collins, P. B. Du Chaillu, Joaquin Miller, Thomas Hughes, Goldwin Smith, James T. Fields, Bishop Doane, Bishop Coxe, Ralph Waldo Emerson, George Bancroft, Edward A. Freeman, Henry C. Carey, and many others equally well known. A few of the journalists to be found among the many are John Walter of the London Times, J. Watson Webb, Morton McMichael, John W. Forney, Wm. Henry Hurlbert, and Whitelaw Reid. But to classify and mention the representative men in the different paths in which they have become celebrated would occupy more space than we have at our command. We can only refer to the names of the Drexels, J. S. Morgan, Governor Cornell, Henry Wilson, Asa Packer, William M. Evarts, General Sherman, General Phil. Sheridan, General McDowell, Sir Stafford Northcote, Robert C. Winthrop, Hamilton Fish, John Welsh, L. P. Morton, Edwards Pierrepont, Earl of Caithness, Samuel J. Tilden, Professor Joseph Henry, Alexander H. Stephens, Rev. Phillips Brooks, Rev. Dr. Henry C. Potter ; but we must stop, not, however, without noting the fact that a very large number of the autographs are accompanied with original sentiments. Dean Stanley adds, alluding to Mr. CHILDS's Memorial Window in Westminster Abbey :—

A grateful farewell to the Angels of Hospitality, and a hope that they may find their way to Westminster Abbey, which will rejoice to receive its munificent benefactor.

Michaelmas, 1878.

Opposite the Dean's remembrance is an original poem by Dean Plumptre. Thomas Nast indicates his appreciation of the humorous in his sketch of himself painting his name, which occupies a page. Oscar Wilde has contributed a poem written in his light flowing hand ; while within a couple of pages is a sentiment by Walt Whitman in his bold, sharp chirography. Lord Houghton has a delicate poem ; Charlotte Cushman and Modjeska each a pleasant thought ; and Lord Dufferin an original poem. Notable especially is the signature of John C. Hamilton, who, as a child, was with his father, Alexander Hamilton, a few hours before he was shot by Burr.

In connection with the Centennial were many foreign celebrities who remember the hospitality of Mr. and Mrs. CHILDS with great pleasure, and among the countries represented by these are China, Egypt, Japan, South America, Australia, and many in Europe. It is needless to say that a volume so full of pleasant memories, and so identified with their lives, is most highly prized by the honored ones who possess it.

Mr. CHILDS has been fortunate enough to secure the original MSS. of Bulwer's "Pilgrims of the Rhine" and "Godolphin." They are splendidly mounted upon large pages, and are arranged in a form worthy of their author. The binding is red levant morocco, richly gilt.

The "Cabinet of the Earl of Derby" is a rich and handsome privately published volume, and was presented by the Duke of Buckingham to Mr. CHILDS. The portraits are fine and true, and, particularly as a study of the men of that time (1871), admirable. The first portrait is that of the Earl of Derby, then follow Lord Chelmsford, Duke of Marlborough, Earl of Malmesbury, D'Israeli, Duke of Buckingham and Chandos, Sir Stafford Northcote, and the other members.

An oddity is "A Collection of the Illustrations of H. K. Browne, better known as 'Phiz.'" Mr. Browne's proper name was first used by the publishers with the "Curiosity Shop," all previous illustrations of books having been under the *sobriquet* of "Phiz." As "Phiz" he is probably best known to the world, and all readers of Dickens's books, and other illustrated works of that time, will remember the spirit and power of his character sketches. This book contains all the sketches, several hundred, that can be obtained, if not all that Mr. Browne ever made; and the collection is enriched by memoranda and notes in his own hand.

We have, in this brief sketch, of course been able only to note the special features of Mr. CHILDS's collection, and we pass by entirely many works that are of great interest.

Were sufficient space at our command many of the rare editions of celebrated works could be described, and many very interesting incidents related concerning them, particularly the presentation copies to which reference has already been made. Of these, all the works of the leading authors of the last twenty years are enriched by the insertion of interesting autograph letters.

In Mr. CHILDS's copy of Dr. Allibone's Dictionary of Authors are many interesting letters from the author, one giving an account of the finishing of the work. Thomas Hartwell Horne, the eminent bibliographer, wrote to Dr. Allibone on the completion of his wonderful Dictionary, commending it in high terms, and said, "Your dedication to Mr. CHILDS is both graceful and grateful."

We cannot close this article, however, without calling attention to an original score of Tom Moore, signed in full.

In addition to this, Mr. CHILDS has numbers of letters, poems, and manuscripts of Burns, Moore, Swift, Longfellow, Bryant, Holmes, Tennyson, Pepys, Pope, Thomson, Shelley, Keats, William Penn, Voltaire, Goethe, Irving, Charles Lamb, Gibbon, Hume, Lord Clarendon, Walter Scott, and others. Coleridge, also, is represented ; and in a long letter he states that he would be glad to go to London if he could be assured of *a guinea a week.* A noteworthy addition is an original manuscript of Schiller—his dramatic poem, entitled "Demetrius." It occupies two folio pages, and was obtained through the kindness of Mr. Longfellow. There is also the original manuscript draft of Tennyson's dedicatory poem to the Queen, which is prefixed to the last collected edition of his poems, and which differs materially from that printed. It is in thirteen verses of four lines each. All the works of the authors named, as well as many others, have the autographs, and steel plates or photographs of the authors.

Without following any exact order we will note a letter of Lord Nelson, written four days before his death ; a number of presentation volumes from the brothers Chambers, Robert, William, and David ; many curiously illustrated inlaid and arranged works, especially Ticknor's Life of Prescott, two volumes, quarto, with several hundred illustrations ; Life of Everett, quarto ; Rogers's Italy and Poems, inlaid with three hundred engravings, all first impressions ; a work on the Empire of Brazil, presented by Dom Pedro in 1876, and containing his autograph ; a copy

of Chambers's "English Literature," which
has autograph letters, about seven hundred
extra plates, and numerous newspaper cuttings and references, the work being extended
to eight volumes; many books upon the North
American Indians ; quite a large collection of
Americana; Lamb's Works, with autograph
letters of Lamb ; Talfourd's Life of Lamb,
with a manuscript poem by Talfourd, and a
letter written to Mr. CHILDS ; Shakspeare's
Works in all the finest editions ; and three
large volumes of photographs, many with
autographs of celebrated people whom Mr.
CHILDS has met within the last quarter of
a century at home and abroad.

Of portraits, in the library, two are especially prominent : one, that of George Pea-
body, full length, who sat for the picture for
Mr. CHILDS ; and the other, that of Mr.
Longfellow, painted by Buchanan Read for
Mr. CHILDS, when the three were spending
the winter of 1868 in Rome together. Both
are admirable portraits, and well adorn the
positions selected for them.

Among the many letters received by Mr.
CHILDS from his friend Mr. Longfellow, the
following, written in regard to his seventieth
birthday, is so characteristic that we print
it : —

CAMBRIDGE, March 13, 1877.

MY DEAR MR. CHILDS:

You do not know yet, what it is to be seventy years old. I will tell you, so that you may not be taken by surprise, when your turn comes.

It is like climbing the Alps. You reach a snow-crowned summit, and see behind you the deep valley stretching miles and miles away, and before you other summits higher and whiter, which you may have strength to climb, or may not. Then you sit down and meditate, and wonder which it will be.

That is the whole story, amplify it as you may. All that one can say is, that life is opportunity.

With seventy good wishes to the dwellers in Walnut Street, corner of Twenty-second,

Yours, very truly,

HENRY W. LONGFELLOW.

There is besides a large, handsome photograph of Dom Pedro, Emperor of Brazil, who sent it with his kindest regards to MR. CHILDS, and whose autograph, with date, appears upon it. That the Emperor has by no means forgotten Mr. CHILDS's hospitalities during the continuation of the Centennial Exhibition is shown by the following brief note which Hon. Thomas A. Osborn, United States Minister to Brazil, writes to a friend, describing his presentation to the Emperor Dom Pedro. He says:—

I have thought that you might not be uninterested in learning that the Emperor, in an informal conversation which followed the presentation of my letter of credence, inquired quite feelingly after Mr. GEORGE W. CHILDS, and manifested a deep concern in his welfare. The Emperor spoke of the hospitalities extended to him in Philadelphia, and was especially warm in his expressions touching Mr. CHILDS.

A number of time-pieces also adorn the library and other parts of the house. There are eighteen in all, one of which, occupying the most prominent position in the drawing-room, cost six thousand dollars. The others are of interest chiefly from the associations connected with them, and for their great age, but are of exceeding beauty, elaborate in design, and ingenious in construction. To these are to be added the large collection of ivories, many of which have been sent to Mr. CHILDS from all parts of the world, and include carvings of rare skill and beauty.

Mr. CHILDS has the original miniature likeness of General Washington which he left by his will to his niece. It is handsomely encased in gold, and contains his hair. Mr. CHILDS obtained from Greenway Court, the estate of the Fairfaxes in Virginia, a handsome mahogany table which General

Washington presented to Lord Fairfax, and on which they often afterwards played cards together. He has also eight old style dining-room chairs which Lord Fairfax brought from Leeds Castle one hundred and fifty years ago.

It is with great regret that we bring this paper to an end. The wealth of material before us is almost confusing, and thrice this space would fail to do full justice to the treasures in the collection ; but we trust some idea may have been given of their value and interest, and that the taste and knowledge of their owner may be appreciated by those who never before heard of the wonderful collection gathered together in the library of Mr. CHILDS. Even those who have had the good fortune to see it and to study its contents, will be glad to read this brief description and to refresh their recollection of such a storehouse of rare, curious, and valuable objects.

www.ingramcontent.com/pod-product-compliance
Lightning Source LLC
Chambersburg PA
CBHW021436090426
42739CB00009B/1504